Karina Kitten's Life Rewritten

A Battle with PTSD

By Carissa Church

Leaning Rock Press

Copyright © 2021 Carissa Church

All rights reserved. No parts of this publication may be reproduced, stored in a database or retrieval system, or transmitted, in any form or by any means, without the prior permission of the publisher or author, except by a reviewer who may quote brief passages in a review.

Leaning Rock Press, LLC
Gales Ferry, CT 06335
leaningrockpress@gmail.com
www.leaningrockpress.com

978-1-950323-48-7, Hardcover
978-1-950323-49-4, Softcover

Library of Congress Control Number: 2021904488


```
Publisher's Cataloging-In-Publication Data
(Prepared by The Donohue Group, Inc.)

Names: Church, Carissa, author.
Title: Karina Kitten's life rewritten : a battle with PTSD / by
   Carissa Church.
Description: Gales Ferry, CT : Leaning Rock Press, [2021] | Series:
   Karina Kitten ; [1] | Includes helpful information and
   statistics about PTSD. | Interest age level: 007-010. | Includes
   bibliographical references. | Summary: "Karina Kitten's father,
   Daddy Kitten, ends up going to the hospital, and the family
   receives news that changes their lives, especially Karina
   Kitten's. Karina Kitten struggles after the change occurs,
   but those around her listen and help her. This ... story of
   animals going through a challenge shows the importance of
   expressing feelings"--Provided by publisher.
Identifiers: ISBN 9781950323487 (hardcover) | ISBN 9781950323494
   (softcover)
Subjects: LCSH: Post-traumatic stress disorder--Juvenile fiction. |
   Families--Mental health--Juvenile fiction. | Emotions--Juvenile
fiction. | Life change events--Psychological aspects--Juvenile
   fiction. | Cats--Juvenile fiction. | CYAC: Post-traumatic stress
   disorder--Fiction. | Families--Mental health--Fiction. | Emo-
tions--Fiction. | Life change events--Psychological aspects--
   Fiction. | Cats--Fiction.
Classification: LCC PZ7.1.C5495 Ka 2021d | DDC [Fic]--dc23
```

Published in the United States of America

Dedication

To my mom and dad.

We have had to go through so much, but we have always had each other. You have done so much for me and let me be me. I love you to the moon and back, and I will always be your little girl.

At 9:00 am on a warm August day, Karina Kitten
and her parents went to her Grandma Cat's house.

Daddy Kitten drove their brand-new car,
and they enjoyed spending time with Grandma Cat.

When Karina Kitten and her parents left Grandma Kitten's house, they went outside and got in the car.

Daddy Kitten drove down the road, and when they got onto a side road, he pulled over.

Once the car stopped, he told Mama Kitten, "My tum is becoming numb."

Karina Kitten became frightened.

She had no clue what was going on.

Daddy Kitten got out of the car and switched seats with Mama Kitten.

Mama Kitten was worried about Daddy Kitten as well and decided to go to Grandma Lynx's house.

When they got inside, Mama Kitten called 911.

Mama Kitten and Grandma Lynx looked frightened.

Daddy Kitten got put in an ambulance and went to the hospital.

After the ambulance left, Mama Kitten told Karina Kitten to go outside and get in the car.

Karina Kitten was worried and confused.

She had no idea what was happening.

Four days later

Mama and Karina Kitten went to visit Daddy Kitten at the hospital.

Karina Kitten was excited to visit Daddy Kitten,
but he was not the same.

He had a bunch of wires and tubes attached to him,
and he was so quiet. He didn't move,
and there was no hair on his head.

Two days after their first visit

Mama and Karina Kitten went back to the hospital.

Mama Kitten and Doctor Rabbit went into the hallway and talked.

Karina Kitten stayed in the room with Daddy Kitten.

He was now able to move and talk again.

It was incredible to spend some time with him.

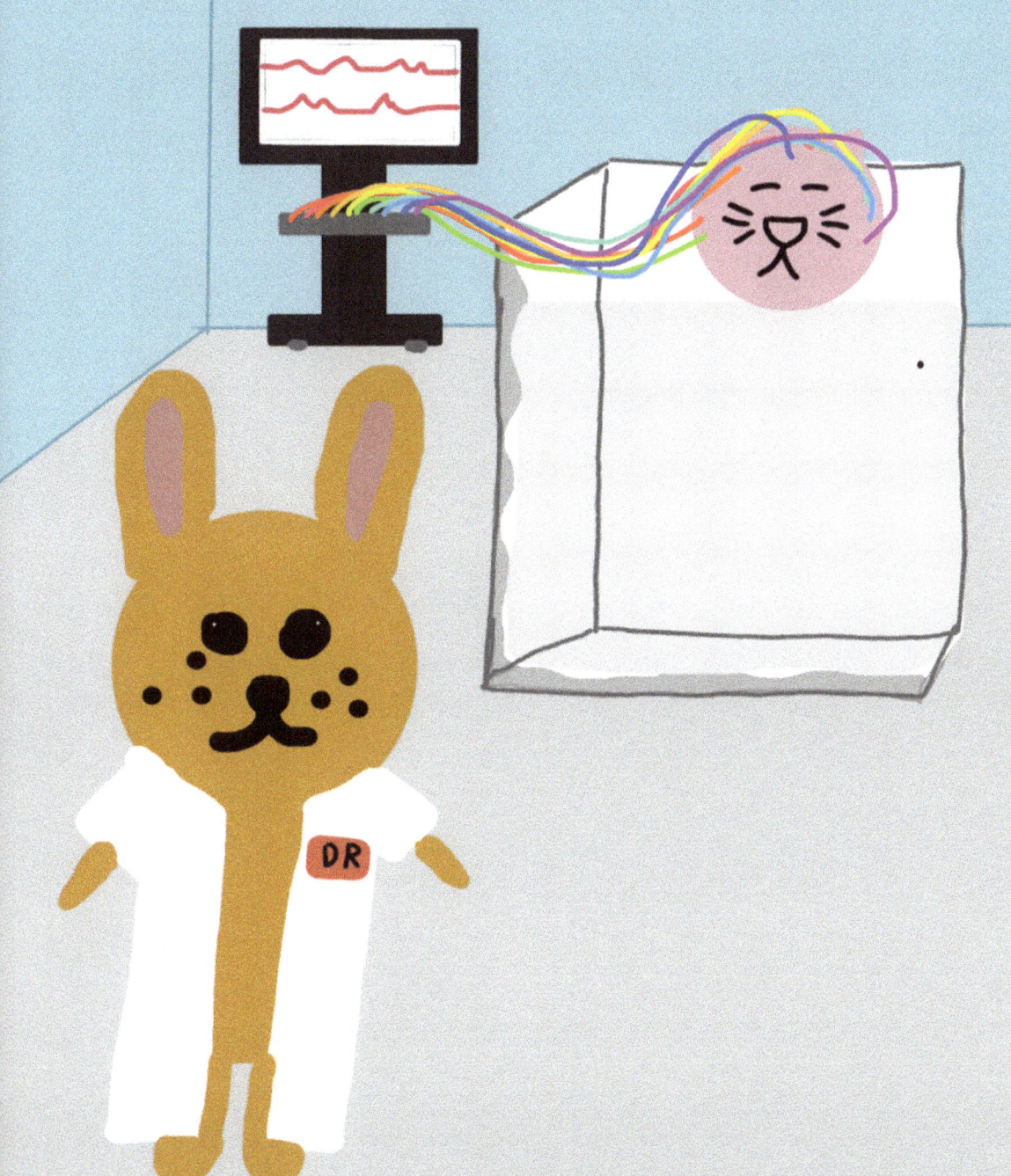

When Mama Kitten and Doctor Rabbit came back into the room,
Doctor Rabbit told Karina Kitten,
"You're getting Daddy Kitten back, and he's going home."

When Karina Kitten understood what was happening,
she was very excited and happy.

Soon they were home, and Karina Kitten was spending
every second with Daddy and Mama Kitten.

Daddy Kitten was better, but he was having many seizures,
panic attacks, and episodes of depression.

In the hospital, they found out that he had had a stroke
and was also diagnosed with epilepsy.

Daddy Kitten, who was in the Army, had seen many bad things.

He now has PTSD.

PTSD stands for:
Post **T**raumatic **S**tress **D**isorder.
It is a mental health condition triggered by a traumatic or terrifying event.
Some symptoms include: reliving the event, avoiding things that remind of the event, increased arousal, as well as negative cognitions and mood.[1,2,4]

Two months pass.

"Hello, Karina Kitten, how are you today?" asked Doctor Owl.

"I am okay, I guess. I can't stop thinking about how scared I was and still am," I said quietly.

"Whenever I see Daddy Kitten have a seizure
or hear someone talk about what happened, I start crying.
The old feelings return. I want things to go back to the way they were.
My family and I have all changed."

> People who experience
> or witness a traumatic event
> may have shock, anger, nervousness,
> fear, and even guilt.[1,3]

"Mama Kitten has told me everything that you have been going through.
We are going to do a few tests to figure out what is going on
so we can help you, Karina Kitten," Doctor Owl nicely stated.

"Ok, thank you," I replied.

The testing took hours.
It consisted of physical exams, psychological evaluation,
and an endless amount of questions.

> To figure out if someone has PTSD,
> most doctors perform a physical exam,
> do a psychological evaluation,
> and use criteria in
> the Diagnostic and Statistical Manual
> of Mental Disorders (DSM-5).
> One sign of PTSD is if you have the symptoms
> and they worsen over time,
> last for months or even years,
> and interfere with your day-to-day life.[3]

Doctor Owl made sure I wasn't sick, and then, the hard tests began.

She showed me many images.
Some gave me stress and made me sad or upset.
She asked me questions
like what causes my sudden mood changes
and what made me stressed.

After the testing, Doctor Owl left the room for almost five minutes
and returned with Mama Kitten.

Doctor Owl asked Mama Kitten and me to sit at her desk.
She then gave us some surprising news.

She told us that I have PTSD, just like Daddy Kitten.

The next few months were very hard.

I felt like I didn't fit in anywhere.
I wanted things to be the way they were before Daddy Kitten got sick.
I barely had any friends because I tried keeping to myself.
No one seemed to understand my struggles besides my parents.

It took me a while to get used to my new life.

I tried fixing things by myself, but eventually,
Doctor Owl had to come in like a superhero.

Because it had been a few months since everything happened, Doctor Owl told us that I should have several months of independent counseling and possibly psychotherapy.

Once I started counseling, life seemed to get better and better. I had more confidence and self-esteem.

I started talking to more people and had a group of friends.

I am so happy that my parents gave me support and got me the help that I needed.

My PTSD is a lot better, but certain images and events still, to this day, are triggers.

A few years later

It has been a couple of years since everything started,
and my parents and I are a lot better.

We are better financially
and have a better relationship with each other.

I now have almost 10 to 15 friends
who I can go to about almost anything.

After everything that happened,
I had to grow up real fast, but I learned a valuable lesson.

When you are feeling down and are struggling,
it is okay to vocalize it and tell others how you feel.

Talking to friends or family will help you and them understand
what you are going through.

Sharing can get rid of the stress that is inside
and allow you to continue understanding and growing.

Recovery is gradual and on-going.
An estimated 7.8 million Americans will
develop PTSD at some point,
but many never get the help they need.
Symptoms often begin within the first
three months, but in some cases,
symptoms don't start until years later.[1,2]

Check out the on-line references for the items in the grey boxes.

1. https://www.webmd.com/mental-health/post-traumatic-stress-disorder#1

2. https://www.mayoclinic.org/diseases-conditions/post-traumatic-stress-disorder/symptoms-cause s/syc-20355967

3. https://www.mayoclinic.org/diseases-conditions/post-traumatic-stress-disorder/diagnosis-treatm ent/drc-20355973

4. https://www.psychiatry.org/patients-families/ptsd/what-is-ptsd

Author and illustrator Carissa Church

Carissa Church lives in Connecticut, and writing is one of her passions. She works hard in school and also plays competitive softball. Currently, she is in high school and is starting to look at colleges. She has gone through many challenges with her family, which help to inspire her books.

Carissa was born with Apraxia of Speech and went through years of speech therapy. When she was 8, her dad had a stroke and was diagnosed with PTSD (Post Traumatic Stress Disorder) from when he was in the United States Army. This event was traumatic for her also and still affects her occasionally. Six years later, he was also diagnosed with epilepsy, and her cat of 11 years passed away. These events compounded the stress she was feeling, giving rise to Carissa's own PTSD symptoms. It is difficult for Carissa to discuss her anxiety and PTSD, which is the driving force behind the message she wants to relay to all: No one should be afraid to express what they are feeling. There will always be someone who will listen and understand what you are going through.

www.ingramcontent.com/pod-product-compliance
Lightning Source LLC
Chambersburg PA
CBHW042016120526
44592CB00044B/2996